Saraswati Panchali

AF519251

Contributions: Aparna Sen Naskar,
Sujata Saha
Purwa Chakraborty
Publisher: DivineBharat

Saraswati Panchali
All Rights Reserved
Contributions: Aparna Sen Naskar,
Sujata Saha
Purwa Chakraborty
Publisher: DivineBharat

ISBN: 978-93-344-3976-2
Email: info@divinebharat.com
Website: www.divinebharat.co
Copyright © 2025 Divinebharat

Index

Introduction

Saraswati Puja, celebrated on Basanta Panchami, is one of the most joyous and spiritually luminous days across Bengal. It falls on the fifth day (Panchami Tithi) of the Shukla Paksha in the month of Magh (January–February). This day is observed as the worship of Goddess Saraswati, the deity of knowledge, wisdom, music, and the arts, while simultaneously marking the arrival of the spring season —a time of new life, colors, and creativity.

Goddess Saraswati is mentioned in the Rigveda, where she is described as the goddess of speech and the divine source of inspiration. Over centuries, this puja has evolved from Vedic rituals into an important cultural and educational festival.

In every Bengali household, Saraswati Puja symbolizes deep devotion and culture. The day is filled with sanctity and joy—the yellow attire, seasonal delicacies, and the gentle fragrance of Shiuli and Palash flowers reflect the renewal of mind and soul.

The puja begins in the morning with bathing and wearing new clothes. Traditionally, yellow garments are worn, symbolizing prosperity and the mustard fields of Bengal in full bloom. The idol or image of Goddess Saraswati is placed on a beautifully decorated altar, adorned with marigolds, Shiuli flowers, and fresh fruits. Children place their books, pens, and musical instruments before the goddess, praying for the blessings of knowledge and wisdom.

Saraswati Puja is one of the most eagerly awaited days for Bengali students. Schools, colleges, and art institutions transform into small temples, decorated with flowers, banana plants, and intricate Alpana designs. Students, dressed in yellow sarees and kurtas, participate in the puja under the guidance of teachers or priests.

Community pandals are set up in towns and villages, symbolizing artistic and cultural unity. This day holds special significance for young children, as it marks the beginning of their education through the “Hate Khori” ceremony—writing their first letters before the goddess, representing the sacred start of learning.

Typical offerings for the puja include khichuri, fried eggplant, kheer, pitha and poli, bananas, sugarcane, and other seasonal items. After the offerings, the prasada is joyfully shared among family, friends, and neighbors.

The “Saraswati Panchali” holds a special place of reverence. Reciting this Panchali during Saraswati Puja is considered highly auspicious.

Puja Materials (Pujar Fardo)

- Sindoor (vermilion)
- 1 set of priest’s ceremonial items (Purohit Baran Samagri)
- Sesame seeds (Til)
- Haritaki
- Panchguli (powdered mixture of five spices)
- Panchgavya (milk, curd, ghee, cow urine, cow dung – used for purification)
- Panchashya (five types of grains or mustard seeds)
- Panchratna (five types of gemstones)
- 1 set of Panchpallav (five types of sacred leaves)

- Ghot (small brass or copper vessel)
- Baran Dala (plate for offerings or welcoming)
- 1 coconut with sprout (Shishta Dhab)
- 1 plate of Atap rice (dry rice for offering)
- Flowers and fruits (Pushpadi) **Palash flower** is dear to the Mother.
- 2 small wooden seats or platforms for the deity (Asan Anguriya)
- 2 bowls for Madhuprekha (mixture of milk, curd, honey, and ghee)
- 2 sets of Naivedya (food offerings)
- 1 set of raw Naivedya (unprocessed food offering)
- Saree for Goddess
- 1 sandalwood garland (Chandramala)
- 1 Bilva leaf garland
- Plate (for Arghya or offerings)

- Conch and cowry-related items (Shankh Kauri)
- Mango buds
- Colored powders for decoration (Abir)
- Fragrant powder (Abeer)
- Ink holder (Moshadhar) – conch or metal container for writing
- Pen or reed pen (Lekhani)
- Bhog (food offerings – fruits, sweets, khichuri, etc.)
- Betel leaves (Paan)
- Betel leaf condiments (supari and other ingredients)
- Kash flower stems (Kashsthal or Kashkand)
- Small quantity of ghee (for rituals)
- 28 Bilva leaves for Homa (fire offerings)
- Camphor (Karpur)
- Dakshina (small monetary and uncooked food offerings on leaf)

Puja Rules

On the day prior to Panchami Tithi, devotees are advised to take simple, pure, and vegetarian food — known as Habishanna Bhojan (food prepared without spices or salt, following religious guidelines).

On the day of Panchami, devotees should wake up early in the morning, take a purifying bath, wear clean and light-colored clothes, and observe a fast.

If an idol (Murti) of Goddess Saraswati is available, it is best to place it and perform the puja. However, if an idol is not available, the puja can be performed using a clay (Mrinmoy) or brass (Pital) pot (Ghat). The pot is filled with Ganga water or any other sacred water.

On the mouth of the pot, a mango leaf (Amapata) is placed, and above it a coconut with sprouts (Shishta Dhab) or a Ramba banana plant (Banana tree) is kept. The pot is decorated with sindoor (vermilion) and placed on a seat made of Atap rice or grains.

At the end of the puja, devotees offer Pushpanjali (flower offerings) to Goddess Saraswati and may then partake in food. Generally, fruits, flattened rice (Chira), milk, and sweets are consumed on this day.

- Eating berries (kul) before the puja is forbidden.

Shri Shri Saraswati Debir Sampurna Puja

1. Achman (Deh Shuddhi)

Sit facing east or north, chant "**Namo Vishnu,**" and sprinkle water in your mouth three times.

Vishnu Smaran Mantra

Om tad Vishnoh paramam padam
sada pashyanti surayah
Divi cha chakshuratatam

Om tad vipraso vipnabo
Jagrubansah samindate
Vishnor yat paramam padam

Purification Mantra

Namah apabitreva pavitro va
sarvavasthang gato'pi va,
yah smaret Pundarikaksham
sa bahyavyantarah shuchih.

Papo'ham papakarma'ham papatma papasambhavah. Trahi maam Pundarikaksha sarvapapam haro Harih.

2. Sankalpa

"**Om Tat Sat Adhya**" If the worshipper is a woman, begin with "**Om Sthaule Namah**"

"**Magh mashe shuklapakshe panchami tithite —Om [bhokter naam] grihite Shri [gotra ba poribarer naam] Devsharma aham Saraswati pratikang Ganapatyadi nana devata puja purbak Saraswati-Lakshmi masayadhare lekhni puja karma aham karishye.**"

3.Bhu Shuddhi

Om Bhumyai Namah. Om Bhumyai Namah. Om Bhumyai Namah.

4.Asana Shuddhi

Om Adhara-shaktaye namah |
Kamalasanaya namah ||
Om asana-mantrasya
Meru-prishtha rishih |
Sutalam chhandah |
Kurmo devata |
Asanopaveshane viniyogah ||

Om prithvi tvaya dhrita loka
Devi tvam Vishnuna dhrita |
Tvam cha dharaya mam nityam
Pavitram kuru chasanam ||

5.Jala Shuddhi

Om Adhara-shaktaye namah |
Om Anantaya namah |
Om Prithvyai namah |
Om Kurmaya namah |
Om Gange cha Yamune chaiva
Godavari Saraswati.
Narmade Sindhu Kaveri
jalehsmin sannidhim kuru.

6.Pushpa Shuddhi

Om pushpe pushpe mahapushpe supushpe pushpasambhave pushpachayabakirne cha hum phat swaha

7.Ghat Sthapana

Om sarvaterthadbhavam bari sarvadeva samanvitam. Imam ghatam samaruhya tishtha devaganaih saha.

8.Ganeshadi Debotar Puja

Om Ganeshaya Namah I
Om Shivaya Namah I
Om Parvatyai Namah I
Om Vishnave Namah I
Om Lakshmyai Namah I
Om Durgayai Namah I
Om Navagrahebhyo Namah I
Om Kuladevatabhyo Namah I
Om Ashtadikpalebhyo Namah II

9.Gandhadi Archana

Upachar (panchopachar orshodashopachar)

Om Gandham Samarpayami I

Om Pushpam Samarpayami I

Om Dhupam Aghrapayami I

Om Dipam Darshayami I

Om Naivedyam Nivedayami I

Om Namah II

Devi Saraswati Dhyan

Om taruna shakalam indo
bibhrati shubhra kantih

kucha bharana mitaangi
sannishanna sitabje

nijakara kamalodya
lekhani pustaka shrih

sakala vibhava siddhyai
patu bagdevata nah

Sri Sri Saraswati Debir Panchali

Saraswati beej mantra
Om Aim Saraswatyai Namah

Narayanam namaskritya
naram chaiva narottamam
Devim Sarasvatim chaiva
tato jayam udirayeta

Pranam janai Saraswati Mayer charane,
Pujen jahake deb asur noro gone.
Jahar kripaye hoy morkho-o gyani,
Asho shuno ebe tar divyo kahini.
Anantshayi Narayan chhilen joganidrate,
Prakriti uday holo tar bama angotheke.
Ek prakriti bade dhore nana rup,
Tahar gyan-roop - Saraswati swaroop.
Bishnur hridoy theke gyan jyoti jage,

Bagdebi bani hetu Brohmar kaje
lage.
Gyaner dhara debi namilo buloke,
Pustakahaste, lohiya honsha bahon
ke.
Swet bastradharini, veenadhari ma,
Bosila tini eshe swet padmasana.
Jeba kore tar puja ei bhumondole,
Chari Ved sarva shastra thake tar
poridhite.
Magh mashe shuklapokkhe
Panchami tithite,
Ghore ghore matake puji bhabbhore
bhoktite.
Shuno ebe shokole, bhokti-jukto
mone,
Kibhabe pujibe tare shastro-bidhi-
gune.
Purbodine hobishanno koribe
grohon,
Panchamir dine sankolpo niye koro
achomon.
Saraswati-name ghot ek koro
sthapon,

Moshadhar lekhoni rakho pujar niyogon.
Ganeshadi panch debe pujibar pore,
Debir puja koro tumi atibhakti bhore.
Naibedya phol je jaha mon chao,
Kshir, misti, pitha-puli diye archan dao.
Bhoktibhore shuddho mone koro debir dhyan,
Saraswati mantro koroho pathon.
Dhup-deep diye arati janao,
Pushpo loye hathe Pushpanjali dayo
Buddhi-vidya shaktir srot tumi anupama,
Bani-madhurya boye jay aloker dhara sama.
Je bhokto puje tare bhokti-jukto hoy,
Chitto jay bhore tar jyaner aloy
He Vidyadayini, koro more uddhar,
Antore probesho ma, ghuchao andhokar.

Shri Saraswatyashtottara Shatanama Stotram

Saraswati Mahabhadra Mahamaya
Baraprada
Shripada Padmanilaya Padmakshi
Padmavaktragaa .. 1 ..
Shivanuja Pustakadhrit Jnanamudra
Rama Para
Kamarupa Mahavidya
Mahapatakanashini .. 2 ..
Mahashraya Malini Cha Mahabhoga
Mahabhuja
Mahabhaga Mahotsaha Divyanga
Surabandita .. 3 ..
Mahakali Mahapasha Mahakara
Mahankusha
Sita Cha Bimala Visha Vidyunmala
Cha Vaishnavi .. 4 ..
Chandrika Chandrabaddana
Chandralekhabhushita

Savitri Sursa Devi Divyalankara
Bhushita .. 5 ..
Bagadevi Vasudha Tibra
Mahabhadra Mahabala
Bhogada Bharati Bhama Govinda
Gomati Shiba .. 6 ..
Jatila Vindhyabasa Cha
Vindhyachalavirajita
Chandika Vaishnavi Brahmi
Brahmajanaik Sadhana .. 7 ..
Soudamini Sudhamurtis Subhadra
Surapujita
Subasini Sunasa Cha Binidra
Padmalocana .. 8 ..
Vidyarupa Vishalakshi Brahmajaya
Mahaphala
Trayimurti Trikalajna Triguna
Shastrarupini .. 9 ..
Shumbhasurapramathini Shubhada
Cha Sarvatmika
Raktabijinihantri Cha Chamunda
Chambika Tatha .. 10 ..

Mundakaya Praharana
Dhumralochana Mardana
Sarvadevastuta Saumya Surasura
Namaskrita .. 11 ..
Kalaratri Kaladhara Rupa
Saubhagyadayini
Bagadevi Cha Bararoha Barahi
Barijasana .. 12 ..
Chitrambrā Chitragandha
Chitramalyabhushita
Kanta Kamaprada Bandhya
Vidyadhara Supujita .. 13 ..
Shvetasana Nilabhuja
Chaturvargaphalaprada
Chaturananasamrajya Raktamadhya
Niranjana .. 14 ..
Hamsasana Nilajangha
Brahmavishnushibatmika
Evam Saraswati Devya
Namnamashtottarashatam .. 15 ..

Iti Shri
Saraswatyashtottarashatanamastotram
Samaptham

Shri Saraswati Prarthana

Ya Kundendu Tusharahara Dhavala
Ya Shubhra Vastravrita
Ya Veena Varadanda Manditakara
Ya Shveta Padmasana
Ya Brahmachyuta Shankara
Prabhritibhir
Devaih Sada Pujita
Sa Mam Pattu Saravatee Bhagavatee
Nihshesha Jadyapaha II 1 II

Shri Saraswati stotra

Shvetabje Shubhravastra Cha
Shveta Gandhanulepana.
Shvetalamkara Bhushadya
Shveta Pushpa Subhasita.
Sa Me Basatu Jihvayam
Bina Pustaka Dharini.
Murari Vallabha Devi
Sarvashukla Saraswati.

Arati

Joy joy banimayer aarati ujjolo।
Mahaanoned nrityo kore
bhoktobrindodol।।
Shonkho baje ghonta baje
baje korotal।
Madhur muridongo baje
parrom roshaal।।
shetoborne debi roupe
gune dhonna।
Aarotite shobha pay
shriradhika konnya।।
Bhoktobrindyo charidheke
horigun gay।
Debir aaroti heri pulok lotai।।
Bosheiayachen binapani
honsobahoney।
Aaroti koriye taar joto debogone।।
Sbashito dhup dip jole monohoro।
E dhorapashe
showbe shebe nirontor।।

Pushpanjali Mantra

O Saraswati mahabhage
bidya kamala lochane I
Bishwarupe bishalakshi
bidhahang dehi Saraswati II

Bhadra-kalyaniye namo nityam,
Saraswatyai namo namah I
Vedo vedango vedanta
vidyashanibhya eva cha II
Esho subh-chandana,
pushpa-bilwa-patra
anjoli Saraswatyai namah II

Saraswati Vandana

Jaya Jaya Devi Chara Chara Share
Kucho Jogo Shobhito Mukta Hare
Beena Ranjita Pustaka Haste
Bhagwati Bharati Devi Namastute

Vidyarambha

Shastraic instruction:

"Maghe masi shuchau pakṣe panchami ya shriyah priya. Tasya purvahnakale tu karyah Sarasvotsavah."

Meaning — On the auspicious Panchami of the Shukla Paksha in the month of Magha, in the early morning, after completing the worship of Goddess Saraswati with flowers, incense, food, and water, it is considered ideal to perform Vidyarambha.

During the Aksharlekha ceremony, a senior family member, guru, or priest holds the child's right hand and recites the Goddess's name:

"**Om namah Sarasvatyai namah.**"

After this, the child is allowed to write the first letter, usually "Om" (**ॐ**) or "Shri" **श्री**

Kshama Prarthana

Avahanam na jaanami
na jaanami tavarchanam |
Poojam chaiva na jaanami
kshamyataam parameshwari ||
Mantraheenam Kriyaheenam
Bhaktiheenam sureshwari |
Yatpoojitam maya devi
paripoornam tadastu me |

VISARJAN

Recite "**Om Sarasvati Devi, Kshamasva**" and perform ghata-chalana (slight movement of the pot).

uttame shikhare devi
bhoomyaam parvata moordhani,
braahmanebhyo hyaujnaanam
gachcha devi yathaa-sukham.
Om gaccha gaccha param sthanam
svasthanam parameshwari
Sangvatsare vyatite tu
punaragamanaya cha

After reciting the mantra, gently move the idol and the ghata slightly and cut the protective thread (bestani sutra).

Shanti-Jal

After the immersion of the murti, bring fresh clean water from the pond, fill the ghata, and sprinkle the water on everyone and around the worship area of the home while reciting:

Om dyauh shantih
Antariksham shantih
Prithvi shantir apah shantih
Oshadhayah shantih
Vanaspatah shantih
Vishvedevah shantih
Brahma shantih
Sarvam shantih
Shantireva shantih
Sa ma shantir edhi
Om shantih shantih shantih

———— iti ————

9 789334 439762

Printed at Repro India Ltd.